THE LEADERSHIP PRAYER INITIATIVE

A GUIDE FOR CHURCHES TO BUILD POWERFUL AND EFFECTIVE PRAYER SUPPORT FOR PASTORS AND MINISTRY LEADERS

CEDAR CREEK MINISTRIES

This resource is designed to equip churches and ministry leaders in cultivating healthy, Scripture-centered prayer for those serving in spiritual leadership. Churches are welcome to share the vision and principles contained within this guide while respecting the integrity of the original work.

Published by **Cedar Creek Ministries**

For additional resources, prayer devotionals, and ministry tools, visit:

Cedar Creek Ministries

www.cedarcreekministries.org

Printed in the United States of America

This prayer initiative is dedicated to ***Kim Martinez****, whose simple desire to make her birthday matter just a little more sparked something far greater than anyone expected.*

What began as a small act of faith—the Prayer Pledge Drive—has grown into a prayer initiative reaching further and touching more lives than we will ever fully see in this life.

Through Kim's heart for prayer and her willingness to begin with something small, the Lord planted seeds of intercession that continue to grow in churches, leaders, and congregations.

One day we will see the eternal fruit of those prayers.

Until then, Cedar Creek Ministries gives thanks for the faithful beginning that helped light the spark.

CONTENTS

Vision & Purpose 7
The Prayer Pledge Drive: Where the Spark Began 8
Why Cedar Creek Ministries Offers Outside Support 11
Common Challenges & Healthy Solutions for Leadership Prayer Teams 15
Biblical Foundation 23
Structure & Leadership of the Prayer Initiative 33
Relational Expectations That Protect Trust 41
Sustainable Rhythms That Help Prayer Initiatives Last 46
The Quiet Power of a Church That Prays for Its Leaders 50
Quick Reference Guide: 54
Simple Encouragement Messages Prayer Teams Can Send 55
Simple Prayer Prompts for Busy Days 56
Signs of a Healthy Prayer Culture 57
Gentle Reminders for Prayer Teams 58

VISION & PURPOSE

Prayer Is the Most Powerful, Biblical, and Accessible Support a Church Can Offer Its Leaders

Scripture describes prayer as a lifeline, a weapon, a shelter, and a ministry of love. Church leaders; pastors, ministry directors, elders, worship leaders, missionaries, staff, and volunteers, carry enormous spiritual, emotional, and relational weight. They face decision fatigue, spiritual warfare, unseen burdens, and seasons of loneliness that very few ever see.

Most churches assume *"someone is praying,"* yet very few congregations cultivate **intentional, consistent, focused prayer on behalf of their leaders.**

This initiative exists to change that.

Our vision is to ignite a long-term, sustainable culture where prayer for church leadership becomes normal, not occasional.

Not reactive.

Not crisis-driven.

But a **daily rhythm** rooted in Scripture, unity, and Spirit-led encouragement.

THE PRAYER PLEDGE DRIVE: WHERE THE SPARK BEGAN

In February,2021, we launched what we thought would be a simple 28-day experiment:

Five people praying for one minute a day for each of the 18 pastors and elders at a single church in Oceanside, California.

That was it...just one focused minute.
No meetings.
No events.
No complicated structure.
Just faithful prayer.

What happened surprised all of us:

- People prayed with more consistency than they ever expected
- Leaders felt seen, supported, and strengthened
- Congregants prayed for pastors they had never personally met
- Spiritual burdens lifted
- Trust grew
- Conversations opened
- A culture of encouragement quietly began to form

Then, when the 28 days ended, two things became unmistakably clear:

The prayer couldn't stop.

God was doing something too significant to treat as a one-month challenge.

At the same time, the enemy pushed back through distraction, discouragement, relational tension, and spiritual resistance.

Instead of deterring us, this confirmed the spiritual reality:

Focused prayer for church leaders is both powerful and spiritually contested.
Which means it is deeply needed.

The Prayer Pledge Drive wasn't the finish line.

It was the spark revealing how deeply pastors need prayer, and how ready congregants are to intercede when they are given clarity, structure, and purpose.

Why This Initiative Exists

This resource is designed to help churches:

- Establish a sustainable, Scripture-centered rhythm of prayer for ministry leaders, inviting God into both the daily work of ministry and times of special need.
- Raise up faithful intercessors and encouragers, forming a trustworthy core group whose consistent prayer can strengthen the culture of a church.
- Strengthen the emotional and spiritual health of leaders by reducing isolation, providing encouragement, and supporting them through faithful prayer.
- Unite the congregation around Christ, cultivating a culture shaped by the fruit of the Spirit; love, joy, peace, patience, kindness, goodness, faithfulness, gentleness, and self-control.

Our heart is not to control, oversee, or run these ministries long-term.
Cedar Creek Ministries exists simply to:

Light the fire.
Equip the saints.
Provide tools, resources, and wisdom.
Help churches begin well and stay healthy.

We have seen trust build slowly, sometimes over years, and that's okay.
Transforming a church culture is a long game.
A prayer culture grows like a tree: seeded in faithfulness, watered by consistency, strengthened by storms, and bearing fruit in due season.

This resource will guide you step-by-step toward creating a safe, biblical, hope-filled environment where leaders are lifted up faithfully—and where congregants discover the joy of interceding for those God has called to shepherd His church.

WHY CEDAR CREEK MINISTRIES OFFERS OUTSIDE SUPPORT

Cedar Creek Ministries is not here to control, oversee, or replace the authority of the local church. Our role is to **come alongside**, offer clarity, share wisdom, and help churches build prayer cultures that last.

Over time, we have seen that an outside partner can gently spark momentum, strengthen trust, and create space for honest communication, especially in churches where leadership has not previously shared prayer needs openly. Many pastors desire prayer but feel hesitant, vulnerable, or unsure how to invite it without placing pressure on their congregation.

Our goal is simple:

to help a church begin well, build wisely, and grow toward healthy, long-term sustainability.

1. A Neutral and Safe Starting Point

An outside ministry provides a gentle kind of neutrality. Because CCM is not part of the church's internal dynamics, both leadership and congregants often feel more comfortable expressing needs, asking questions, and discussing hopes for the prayer initiative.

This creates a foundation of trust, not pressure, at the beginning.

2. Encouragement Without Internal Expectations

Church leaders sometimes carry hidden hesitations:

- "If I share this, will it burden someone?"
- "Will people misunderstand?"
- "Will prayer turn into a critique session?"
- "Will this become emotional or complicated?"

With outside support, pastors can begin sharing prayer needs appropriately and confidently, knowing the group is being equipped with tools for confidentiality, encouragement, and biblical prayer.

3. Tools, Structure, and Resources Churches Don't Have to Create Alone

Most churches want to pray consistently for their leaders but don't have the time or staff capacity to build:

- training materials
- prayer calendars
- expectations sheets
- communication processes
- sustainable rhythms
- healthy relational guidelines
- rotation systems
- encouragement tools

CCM simply provides these resources so each church can adapt them to its own culture and people.

We do not stay forever.
We simply **light the fire** and hand the church everything needed to carry it forward.

4. Support for Healthy Relational Dynamics

By offering biblical guidance on:

- Confidentiality
- propriety
- appropriate encouragement
- same-gender spiritual support
- avoiding emotional entanglement
- cultivating a culture of kindness and honor
- Cultivating the gifts of edification

CCM helps prayer teams begin with wisdom, protecting marriages, guarding hearts, and keeping the focus on Christ and His calling on church leadership.

We do not introduce fear-based rules.
We simply provide **biblical, practical frameworks** that help men and women serve with purity, integrity, and joy.

5. Sustainability Through Seasons of Change

When churches rely solely on one or two internal champions, prayer efforts often fade when life transitions occur; people move, ministry seasons shift, or volunteers change roles.

By helping churches build clear, simple structure from the beginning, CCM supports the creation of a prayer culture that lasts:

- through staff transitions
- through elder rotations
- through ministry busy seasons
- through cultural shift
- through growth

The goal is always to bless the church with something steady, unified, and sustainable.

In Summary

Cedar Creek Ministries exists to strengthen the local church by:

- igniting intentional prayer
- equipping saints with tools and structure
- encouraging leaders
- promoting biblical unity
- protecting relational health
- and helping every church become a place where prayer is woven into the culture itself

We spark the flame.
You carry it forward.
And God receives the glory.

COMMON CHALLENGES & HEALTHY SOLUTIONS FOR LEADERSHIP PRAYER TEAMS

Even in loving, Christ-centered churches, prayer efforts can drift without guidance. These challenges are normal, not signs of dysfunction, but they provide opportunities for wisdom, clarity, and growth.

We have added a simple **Problem → Solution** framework that will help every church begin in strength and stay healthy long-term.

1. Problem: Internal Dynamics Can Make Leaders Hesitant

Leaders often wonder:

- "Will this burden someone?"
- "Will my request be misunderstood?"
- "Will people assume something is wrong?"
- "Will this become emotional or complicated?"

These normal hesitations can make pastors slow to share prayer needs.

Solution: A Gentle, Neutral Starting Place

With outside support, leaders feel safer expressing needs without pressure or politics. This builds trust slowly, naturally, and biblically.

2. Problem: Prayer Requests Sometimes Drift Into Venting

Without focus, prayer moments can unintentionally become:

- Frustration-sharing
- Rumors
- Speculation
- personal opinions wrapped in spiritual language

It's rarely malicious, just human nature.

Solution: Clear Biblical Focus and Simple Structure

When prayer is directed toward Scripture, encouragement, and specific prompts, conversations stay:

- Christ-centered
- Uplifting
- Safe
- Edifying
- aligned with the fruit of the Spirit

A simple structure keeps prayer pure and purposeful.

3. Problem: Emotional Over-Connection Can Develop

Prayer creates closeness quickly.
Without guidance, people may:

- become overly attached
- feel responsible for a leader's emotions
- interpret spiritual closeness as relational closeness
- blur propriety without realizing it

This creates pressure for leaders and vulnerability for all.

Solution: Healthy, Biblical Relational Expectations

CCM helps prayer teams cultivate:

- propriety without fear
- encouragement without emotional dependence
- group-based prayer instead of isolated moments
- same-gender spiritual support for deeper matters

This protects marriages, hearts, reputations, and the integrity of the ministry.

4. Problem: Participants May Feel They've Gained Influence

Sometimes people genuinely think that praying for leaders gives them:

- a voice in decisions
- special insight
- spiritual authority
- leadership influence

Not out of pride, often out of passion.

Solution: Reinforcing the Purpose of Intercession

CCM's tools help prayer teams embrace their *true* calling:

- Encouragement
- Support
- Intercession
- protecting leaders
- strengthening unity in the church

Not steering decisions.
Not influencing direction.
Just faithfully praying.

5. Problem: Everything Can Accidentally Land on the Pastor's Wife

Without guidance, churches often funnel:

- emotional burdens
- Questions
- Updates
- concerns

to the pastor's wife...leaving her carrying the weight of the prayer team.

Solution: Clear Structure & Shared Responsibility

We help churches set up:

- simple communication flows
- shared leadership
- clarity around who carries what
- group prayer rhythms

...so no single person becomes the default emotional hub.

6. Problem: Prayer Efforts Fade When Seasons Change

When a ministry relies on one or two passionate people, it often collapses if life shifts:

- someone moves
- someone gets discouraged
- someone gets sick
- someone becomes overwhelmed
- someone takes on new responsibilities

Beautiful ministry fades, not because of lack of heart, but lack of structure.

Solution: Build a Sustainable Rhythm From the Beginning

CCM offers:

- rotation systems
- prayer calendars
- clear expectations
- simple training
- long-game vision

so the prayer culture continues regardless of seasonal transitions.

A Better Way Forward

These challenges are not reasons to fear. They're simply invitations to begin wisely.

With gentle outside support, biblical clarity, and simple tools, churches can build leadership prayer teams that are:

- Healthy
- Trustworthy
- Sustainable
- Uplifting
- Christ-centered
- culturally safe
- spiritually powerful

And the fruit lasts for years.

BIBLICAL FOUNDATION

A leadership prayer initiative must be built on Scripture. Initiatives can not be built on trends, emotion, or human effort alone. Throughout church history, spiritual vitality has always flowed through praying people who believed God hears, responds, and sustains His servants through intercession.

This section lays the biblical groundwork that shapes everything that follows. These verses and historic voices remind us that prayer is not a small act. Prayer is a kingdom act, a culture-shifting act, and one of the most accessible ministries every believer can enter.

1. Prayer & Intercession Are Biblical Commands

Throughout Scripture, God calls His people to lift up those in places of spiritual responsibility.

> *"I urge that supplications, prayers, intercessions, and thanksgivings be made for all people... for kings and all who are in high positions."*
>
> — 1 TIMOTHY 2:1–2

Application:

Praying for leaders is not a suggestion. It is a priority. God ties the health of a community to the intercession of its people.

> *"Praying at all times in the Spirit, with all prayer and supplication..."*
>
> — EPHESIANS 6:18

Application:

Prayer is continual, Spirit-led, flexible, and adaptable—exactly what your prayer initiative models.

> *"The effective, fervent prayer of a righteous man avails much."*
>
> — JAMES 5:16

Application:

Even **one minute** of focused prayer (like the PPD) carries weight in heaven. God moves through simple, faithful, steady prayer.

> *"...always struggling on your behalf in his prayers, that you may stand mature and fully assured in all the will of God."*
>
> — COLOSSIANS 4:12

Application:

A biblical prayer warrior is someone who wants to see leaders stand strong, mature, confident, and aligned with God's will.

> *"I appeal to you, brothers, by our Lord Jesus Christ and by the love of the Spirit, to strive together with me in your prayers to God on my behalf."*
>
> — ROMANS 15:30

> *"You also must help us by prayer, so that many will give thanks on our behalf for the blessing granted us through the prayers of many."*
>
> — 2 CORINTHIANS 1:11

Paul repeatedly appeals for prayer as essential to his ministry.

Application:

The greatest church planter in history acknowledged his dependence on the prayers of ordinary believers. Leaders today are no different.

2. Encouragement Is a Biblical Ministry

Prayer is not only intercession. Prayer is encouragement in action.

> *"Therefore encourage one another and build one another up..."*
>
> — THESSALONIANS 5:11

Application:

Your prayer initiative is a ministry of building up, not tearing down; strengthening, not critiquing.

> *"The Lord God has given me the tongue... to know how to sustain with a word him who is **Dedication***
>
> *This prayer initiative is dedicated to **Kim Martinez**, whose simple desire to make her birthday matter just a little more sparked something far greater than anyone expected.*
>
> *What began as a small act of faith—the Prayer Pledge Drive—has grown into a prayer initiative reaching further and touching more lives than we will ever fully see in this life.*
>
> *Through Kim's heart for prayer and her willingness to begin with something small, the Lord planted seeds of intercession that continue to grow in churches, leaders, and congregations.*
>
> *One day we will see the eternal fruit of those prayers.*
>
> *Until then, Cedar Creek Ministries gives thanks for the faithful beginning that helped light the spark.*
>
> *weary."*
>
> — ISAIAH 50:4

Application:

Encouragers hold a sacred role, lifting weary leaders with a word, a prayer, or a moment of steady intercession.

> *"Anxiety in a man's heart weighs him down, but a good word makes him glad."*
>
> — PROVERBS 12:25

Application:

Prayer brings gladness to leaders weighed down by unseen burdens.

3. Supporting Spiritual Leaders Is a Biblical Responsibility

Scripture does not shy away from calling the church to honor and uphold its leaders.

> *"...for they are keeping watch over your souls."*
>
> — HEBREWS 13:17

Application:

Praying for leaders is one of the most loving ways to support those who carry the weight of shepherding souls.

> *"Esteem them very highly in love because of their work."*
>
> — 1 THESSALONIANS 5:12–13

Application:

Honoring leaders includes interceding for their strength, families, decisions, and perseverance.

> *As long as Moses held up his hands, Israel prevailed... Aaron and Hur held up his hands.*
>
> — EXODUS 17:11–12

Application:

This is the heartbeat of your prayer initiative:

Leaders are strengthened when faithful people hold up their arms.

4. Perseverance, Unity & Spiritual Warfare

Prayer holds the line in seasons of spiritual resistance.

> *"We prayed to our God and set a guard..."*
>
> — NEHEMIAH 4:9

Application:

Prayer is not passive—it is watchful, wise, and protective.

> *"So Peter was kept in prison, but earnest prayer for him was made to God by the church."*
>
> — ACTS 12:5

Application:

Leaders need earnest prayer in both crisis and normal ministry life. God moves through praying congregations.

5. Voices From Church History Who Emphasize Prayer's Power

Theologians and pastors throughout history affirm what Scripture teaches: **prayer is the lifeblood of the church and the strength of its leaders.**

Charles Spurgeon (1834–1892)

The Preacher Who Built a Ministry on Prayer

Spurgeon pastored thousands, preached globally, and trained pastors, but he consistently said the real power of his ministry came from the intercessors who prayed beneath the sanctuary.

Quote:

> *"I would rather teach one man to pray than ten men to preach."*

Application:

Prayer is not secondary. Prayer is foundational.

E.M. Bounds (1835–1913)

The Pastor Who Believed Prayer Was the Real Work

E.M. Bounds wrote his books on prayer before dawn, believing prayer was not preparation for ministry. It was the ministry. His theology reminds us that God doesn't need better systems; He desires deeper prayer.

Quote:

> *"The church is looking for better methods; God is looking for better men of prayer."*

Application:

Your initiative isn't about methods, but faithfulness.
Not about more programs, but more intercession.

Andrew Murray (1828–1917)

The Pastor Who Taught the Church to Abide

Andrew Murray emphasized abiding, surrender, and partnership with God through prayer. He believed prayer was how ordinary believers joined God in His work in the world.

Quote:

> *"The man who mobilizes the Christian church to pray will make the greatest contribution to world evangelization in history."*

Application:

Your prayer team is part of something eternal, global, and profoundly impactful, even when it feels quiet and unseen.

Bringing It All Together

Scripture, history, and experience all teach the same truth:

God moves when His people pray.
Leaders stand stronger when congregations intercede.
Church cultures shift when prayer becomes part of the rhythm of daily life.

This initiative is not about perfection...it is about faithfulness.
Not about emotion...it is about consistency.
Not about pressure...it is about invitation.

Your prayer team begins with the Word, is strengthened by the stories of saints who have gone before, and grows through simple, faithful obedience to Christ.

STRUCTURE & LEADERSHIP OF THE PRAYER INITIATIVE

A prayer initiative flourishes when it begins with simplicity, clarity, and flexibility. Churches do not need complicated systems or weekly meetings to cultivate faithful intercession. They simply need a framework that supports consistency, protects relational health, and empowers people to pray in ways that fit their daily rhythms.

This section provides a flexible, biblical structure that any church, large or small, traditional or contemporary can adapt to its own culture.

1. A Simple, Sustainable Leadership Structure

Every prayer initiative needs leadership, but not heavy leadership.

The goal is to empower, not overwhelm.

A healthy structure includes:

A. A Pastor or Elder Sponsor

Someone from the leadership team who:

- Offers direction and clarity
- Shares appropriate prayer needs
- Encourages transparency
- Helps build trust over time

They do NOT run the group.
They simply provide connection and support.

B. A Prayer Team Coordinator

One trusted congregant who:

- Communicates updates
- Distributes prayer prompts
- Maintains rotation schedules
- Encourages the group
- Serves as the point of contact

This does not need to be a "big commitment" role, just someone steady and joyful.

C. The Prayer Team (8–12 People)

This is the heart of the initiative.

A small group is intentional:

- big enough to cover needs
- small enough to stay connected
- flexible enough to adapt
- intimate enough to maintain trust

These intercessors pray from Scripture, pray with unity, and pray with confidentiality.

2. Multiple Ways to Pray (Flexible Models for Busy Lives)

Prayer does not need to be a weekly gathering.

In fact, the most sustainable models are simple, consistent, and woven into daily routines.

Here are multiple structures a church may choose from and most congregations use a combination.

A. Focused Calendars (Monthly or Quarterly)

A prayer calendar provides:

- Scripture-based prompts
- specific topics
- Consistency
- unity of focus

For example:

- Week 1: Pastoral family
- Week 2: Spiritual direction & clarity
- Week 3: Staff unity
- Week 4: Outreach, discipleship, community impact

This model works beautifully for busy churches.

B. Prayer Devotional Booklets (31-Day Prayer Devotionals)

A prayer devotional booklet provides:

- Scripture-centered encouragement
- a short daily devotional thought
- a focused daily prayer
- a simple rhythm that builds consistent prayer habits
- unity across individuals, small groups, and congregations

Each booklet contains 31 days of guided prayer, making it an excellent starting point for churches launching a prayer initiative.

For example:

- Week 1: The spiritual life of your pastor
- Week 2: Wisdom in leadership and preaching
- Week 3: Family strength and protection

- Week 4: Endurance, joy, and fruitful ministry

Current devotionals include:

- Pray for Your Pastor — A 31-Day Prayer Devotional
- Pray for Your Pastor's Wife — A 31-Day Prayer Devotional

These devotionals serve as an excellent on-ramp for a prayer initiative, helping churches establish a steady rhythm of praying for their leaders.

C. Daily "One Minute" Intercession

Inspired by the Prayer Pledge Drive.

Even the busiest person can pray for:

- 60 seconds
- one leader a day
- one Scripture
- one request
- one blessing

This model creates long-term consistency and removes pressure or guilt.

D. Scheduled Rhythms (No Meetings Required)

Many churches choose a "pray at the same time" model:

- Every morning at 7am
- Mondays at noon
- Daily at 9pm
- Fridays on the drive to work

They never meet in person, but they pray in unity.

E. Digital Prayer Connections

Ideal for younger congregations, commuters, parents, or people with irregular schedules.

Examples:

- WhatsApp group
- Group text
- Email chain
- Church app
- Slack or Messenger
- Zoom prayer once a month

These allow:

- quick prompts
- immediate Scripture sharing
- encouragement
- anonymity when needed
- accessibility for all ages

F. Small Group or Ministry-Specific Coverage

Some churches assign prayer partners to:

- worship team
- children's ministry
- youth leaders
- elders
- pastoral staff
- missionaries

Each intercessor adopts a ministry (or a person) for a season.

This builds deep, consistent support.

3. What a Prayer Time Can Look Like

Here are simple examples for churches to choose from:

A. The 5-Minute Model

1. **Stillness** (10 seconds)
2. **Scripture** (choose one from the prayer calendar or devotional journal)
3. **Pray for one leader**
4. **Pray for unity & fruit of the Spirit**
5. **Pray for God's presence to guide the church**

Consistent. Simple. Sustainable.

B. The 10-Minute Rotation Model

- 2 minutes — worship & gratitude
- 2 minutes — Scripture reading
- 2 minutes — leadership focus
- 2 minutes — church-wide needs
- 2 minutes — blessing & encouragement

C. Monthly Group Prayer (In-Person or Zoom)

A 20–30 minute optional meeting:

- brief Scripture
- a short update
- silent prayer or guided prayer
- group encouragement
- close with a blessing

This meeting is optional, not foundational.

4. Roles Within the Prayer Team

Each prayer team is strengthened by members with distinct giftings. Examples:

- **Encouragers**: send notes or Scriptures
- **Intercessors**: pray privately and consistently
- **Scripture Readers**: share passages in the group chat
- **Communicators**: send weekly prompts
- **Quiet Faithful Ones**: show up, pray, and hold the line

A healthy team honors all of these gifts equally.

5. The Heart Beneath the Structure

The structure is not the goal.

The goal is:

- **Faithfulness**
- **Unity**
- **Kindness**
- **Consistency**
- **Safety**
- **Trust**
- **Encouragement**
- **God's presence in the details**

Structure simply creates a rhythm where those things can grow.

6. Setting the Stage for the Expectations Section

Before building out expectations (next section), remember:

- Prayer is relational, not organizational
- Trust takes time
- Leaders need safe people
- Encouragement is a ministry
- Prayer protects, strengthens, and restores
- This is a long-game culture shift
- Small, steady steps matter

RELATIONAL EXPECTATIONS THAT PROTECT TRUST

Every healthy ministry thrives when expectations are clear, simple, and rooted in Scripture.

Prayer teams are not built on rules, but they do benefit from shared commitments that protect relationships, guard hearts, and keep the focus on Christ. These expectations create an environment where leaders feel safe to receive prayer and where intercessors can serve with freedom and joy.

Healthy expectations prevent misunderstandings before they begin and help the prayer initiative remain a ministry of encouragement rather than pressure.

Below are several guiding principles that help prayer teams remain spiritually healthy and relationally wise.

1. Prayer Is the Primary Calling

The purpose of the prayer initiative is exactly what the name suggests: prayer.

Prayer team members are not advisors, counselors, or decision-makers. Their role is to faithfully bring leaders before the Lord, asking for wisdom, protection, endurance, and joy in ministry.

The ministry of intercession is powerful precisely because it places the work in God's hands rather than our own.

Prayer teams exist to lift leaders up to the Lord, not to shape their leadership.

2. Confidentiality Builds Safety

Trust grows when people know their words will be handled with care.

Prayer requests shared within the prayer team should remain within that circle unless leaders clearly indicate otherwise. This protects reputations, guards sensitive information, and creates a space where leaders feel comfortable sharing genuine needs.

Confidentiality does not mean secrecy or isolation. It simply means prayer requests are handled with wisdom, discretion, and respect.

A culture of confidentiality strengthens both the prayer team and the leaders they serve.

3. Encouragement Should Always Outweigh Criticism

The tone of a leadership prayer initiative should always be uplifting, gracious, and hope-filled.

Prayer team members intentionally look for ways to strengthen leaders through encouragement, whether through prayer, a Scripture text, or a kind word.

The goal is not to analyze leadership decisions or discuss church dynamics. The goal is to build up the people God has called to shepherd the church.

Encouragement is a ministry in itself, and it often becomes one of the most meaningful fruits of the prayer initiative.

4. Prayer Does Not Grant Influence

Sometimes people assume that praying for leaders provides a special voice in leadership decisions. Scripture, however, teaches something different.

Intercession strengthens leadership but does not steer it.

Prayer team members serve by supporting leaders spiritually, not by shaping ministry direction. This posture protects unity within the church and keeps the focus on the spiritual calling of prayer.

When prayer remains humble and supportive, the entire church benefits.

5. Healthy Priorities Protect Everyone

Prayer builds spiritual closeness, and healthy ministries steward that closeness with wisdom and care.

Encouragement is a beautiful and biblical ministry within the body of Christ. Scripture calls believers to build one another up, and many faithful men and women are gifted in the ministry of encouragement and edification. Notes, messages, Scripture reminders, and simple words of gratitude can strengthen leaders in powerful ways. These expressions of encouragement are welcomed and valued.

At the same time, a healthy prayer initiative encourages prayer to take place primarily in group settings or through shared prayer rhythms rather than isolated, emotionally intense interactions. This keeps the focus on intercession while maintaining a culture of wisdom, respect, and relational health.

Within this framework, men and women alike are free to use their gifts to pray, encourage, and build up the leaders God has called to shepherd His church.

These priorities help create an environment where both leaders and intercessors can serve with confidence, integrity, and peace.

6. The Initiative Belongs to the Whole Church

While a small prayer team may serve as the core of the initiative, the long-term goal is a church culture where praying for leaders becomes normal and natural for the entire congregation.

Some members may pray daily.
Others may follow a monthly prayer calendar.
Others may join occasional prayer gatherings.

Every prayer matters.

A healthy prayer culture grows slowly, spreading through relationships, encouragement, and shared spiritual rhythms.

7. Grace and Flexibility Matter

No prayer initiative will run perfectly.

People will miss days.
Schedules will shift.
Leadership needs will change.

That is normal.

The goal is not perfection. The goal is faithfulness.

When prayer teams extend grace to one another and remain focused on Christ, the initiative becomes sustainable for years rather than exhausting in months.

With these expectations in place, the next step is to establish simple rhythms that help prayer teams remain steady over time.

In the following section we will explore practical ways churches can maintain sustainable prayer rhythms, share responsibilities wisely, and continue strengthening leaders through faithful intercession.

SUSTAINABLE RHYTHMS THAT HELP PRAYER INITIATIVES LAST

A leadership prayer initiative is not meant to be a short-term project or a burst of enthusiasm that fades after a few weeks. Its purpose is to cultivate a steady culture of intercession that quietly strengthens leaders over months and years.

Healthy prayer cultures grow through rhythm, not pressure. They are built through consistent, manageable practices that allow people to participate faithfully without becoming overwhelmed. When prayer is woven into normal life rather than treated as an extra obligation, it becomes sustainable for the long term.

The following rhythms help many churches maintain steady, faithful intercession while protecting the health of both leaders and prayer team members.

1. Consistency Matters More Than Intensity

Many prayer efforts begin with strong enthusiasm but unintentionally place too much pressure on participants. Long meetings, complicated schedules, or constant updates can eventually discourage even faithful people.

A sustainable prayer initiative focuses on consistency rather than intensity.

One minute of prayer each day.
A short Scripture shared once a week.
A simple reminder to pray for a leader.

These small rhythms accumulate into powerful spiritual support over time. Steady prayer often carries greater long-term impact than occasional bursts of activity.

Faithfulness, not volume, is what sustains the ministry.

2. Shared Responsibility Strengthens the Initiative

When prayer initiatives depend on one or two passionate individuals, they often struggle when life circumstances change. Healthy prayer cultures distribute responsibility so that the ministry does not depend on a single person.

This may include:

- a coordinator who sends prayer prompts
- someone who shares Scripture with the group
- others who occasionally send encouragement
- participants who quietly pray each day
- Each role contributes to the overall strength of the prayer initiative.
- Shared participation allows the ministry to continue through transitions, busy seasons, and changes in church leadership.

3. Simple Communication Keeps Prayer Focused

Prayer teams benefit from clear and gentle communication. Updates do not need to be frequent or detailed. Often a short prompt is enough to keep the group unified in prayer.

Many churches choose to share:

- a weekly prayer focus
- a Scripture passage
- one or two specific requests

- Use a premade devotional

Digital tools such as group messages, email updates, or church apps can make these reminders easy to distribute.

The goal is not to create constant conversation, but to quietly guide the prayers of the group toward the needs of church leadership.

4. Prayer Rhythms Can Follow the Life of the Church

Many churches find it helpful to align prayer rhythms with the natural seasons of ministry.

For example:

- one week may focus on pastoral families
- another week on wisdom for leadership decisions
- another on staff unity and spiritual strength
- another on outreach, discipleship, and community impact

These rhythms allow prayer teams to intercede for leaders in a way that reflects the real life of the church.

Seasonal prayer also helps intercessors remain engaged because the focus naturally shifts throughout the year.

5. Encouragement Is One of the Most Meaningful Fruits of Prayer

While prayer itself is the foundation of this initiative, encouragement often becomes one of its most visible and powerful outcomes.

- A short message expressing gratitude for a sermon.
- A Scripture sent to a pastor before a busy week.
- A note thanking a ministry leader for faithful service.

These simple acts remind leaders that they are not serving alone.

Encouragement does not need to be elaborate. Often a single sincere word can lift a weary heart and strengthen a leader's resolve to continue serving.

6. Grace Allows the Initiative to Continue for Years

Every prayer initiative will experience seasons of adjustment. Participants may move away, leadership teams may change, and ministry rhythms may shift.

These changes are normal.

When prayer initiatives operate with grace rather than rigid expectations, they adapt naturally to new seasons. The goal is not to maintain a perfect structure, but to keep prayer alive within the church.

Over time, faithful intercession begins to shape the culture of the congregation itself. Prayer for leaders becomes normal, expected, and deeply valued.

And when that happens, the church begins to experience the quiet strength that comes when leaders are consistently lifted before the Lord.

As prayer becomes woven into the rhythm of church life, the impact extends far beyond the initial group of intercessors.

In the next section, we will explore how churches can continue strengthening this culture through encouragement, unity, and shared participation across the congregation.

THE QUIET POWER OF A CHURCH THAT PRAYS FOR ITS LEADERS

Healthy prayer initiatives rarely begin with large numbers or dramatic moments. Most begin quietly, with a small group of faithful believers who simply decide to pray.

Over time, something beautiful begins to grow.

1. Leaders feel supported in ways they may not always be able to explain.
2. Congregants develop a deeper affection for those who shepherd them.
3. Encouragement becomes more natural.
4. Unity grows stronger.
5. Prayer becomes woven into the life of the church.

None of this happens through pressure or programs. It grows through steady faithfulness.

A church that prays for its leaders becomes a church marked by kindness, humility, and trust. The atmosphere shifts. Conversations change. Spiritual resilience strengthens.

Pastors and ministry leaders often carry responsibilities that few people fully see. When a congregation commits to praying for them consistently, the church participates in strengthening the very people God has called to guide, teach, and care for His people.

The work of intercession may feel quiet, but its impact is profound.

Faithfulness Matters More Than Perfection

No prayer initiative will ever run perfectly.

Some weeks the prayers will be brief.
Some seasons will be quieter than others.
Participants may come and go.

This is normal.

The strength of a prayer initiative is not found in flawless organization but in simple faithfulness. When believers continue bringing their leaders before the Lord, even in small ways, God uses those prayers to sustain and strengthen His church.

The Invitation Before You

Every church can cultivate a culture of prayer for its leaders.

It does not require a large staff.
It does not require elaborate programs.
It simply requires willing hearts.

A small group of faithful intercessors can begin the shift.

Eight people praying.
A Scripture shared each week.
A quiet word of encouragement sent to a leader.

These simple acts become seeds that God grows over time.

A Final Encouragement

Scripture reminds us that leaders are strengthened through the prayers of God's people.

> *"You also must help us by prayer..."*
>
> — 2 CORINTHIANS 1:11

The Apostle Paul, one of the most influential leaders in the history of the church, openly asked ordinary believers to pray for him. He understood that ministry is never meant to be carried alone.

The same is true today.

When a church lifts its leaders in prayer, it participates in the work God is doing through them.

Prayer strengthens.
Prayer protects.
Prayer encourages.
Prayer sustains.

And through faithful intercession, the entire church is blessed.

Remember...

If your church is beginning this journey... start simply

Gather a few trusted people.
Share the vision.
Choose a rhythm that fits your congregation.
Pray faithfully.

Over time, the culture of the church will begin to reflect what Scripture has always taught:

God strengthens His people when they pray for one another.

QUICK REFERENCE GUIDE:

Phrases That Help Shape a Prayer Culture

Leaders and prayer coordinators often need simple language that keeps conversations healthy and Christ-centered.

These short phrases help redirect discussions toward encouragement and prayer.

Helpful Culture-Shaping Phrases

- "Let's turn that into a prayer."
- "How can we pray for them this week?"
- "Let's assume the best and pray for wisdom."
- "Our role is to support our leaders in prayer."
- "Prayer strengthens leaders; it doesn't steer them."
- "Encouragement builds the church."
- "Let's pray Scripture over that."
- "We don't need every detail to pray faithfully."
- "God sees what leaders carry even when we don't."
- "Faithful prayer often works quietly but powerfully."

These phrases help keep the atmosphere focused on **prayer rather than analysis.**

SIMPLE ENCOURAGEMENT MESSAGES PRAYER TEAMS CAN SEND

Many people want to encourage leaders but don’t know what to say.

Short messages like these help make encouragement natural.

Examples:

- “We prayed for you this morning. Thank you for faithfully shepherding our church.”
- “May the Lord give you wisdom and peace as you lead this week.”
- “Grateful for the way you serve our church family.”
- “Praying for strength and joy in your ministry this week.”
- “Your leadership matters more than you probably realize.”

Even brief messages can lift a leader’s heart.

SIMPLE PRAYER PROMPTS FOR BUSY DAYS

For moments when people want to pray but need a starting point. These are examples, to get you going or keep you going when days feel heavy.

A One-Minute Prayer

> *"Lord, give our leaders wisdom, strength, protection, and joy as they serve Your church today."*

A Scripture Prayer

> *"Lord, help our leaders stand mature and fully assured in all Your will."*

Colossians 4:12

A Blessing Prayer

> *"May the Lord guide, protect, and strengthen those who shepherd this church."*

SIGNS OF A HEALTHY PRAYER CULTURE

Over time, a church may notice small shifts that show prayer is taking root.

Healthy signs include:

- Leaders feel supported rather than scrutinized
- Encouragement increases across the church
- Prayer becomes a normal response to challenges
- Congregants speak about leaders with honor
- Unity strengthens during difficult seasons
- Spiritual conversations become more natural

These are quiet but powerful indicators that prayer is shaping the culture.

GENTLE REMINDERS FOR PRAYER TEAMS

A short page of reminders can keep the initiative centered on its purpose.

Remember:

- Prayer is the ministry.
- Encouragement strengthens leaders.
- Faithfulness matters more than intensity.
- Prayer does not grant influence.
- We pray because we love the church and its leaders.
- God is the one who brings the fruit.

Cedar Creek Ministries prays, the Lord gives your leaders wisdom in every decision, strength in every season, joy in their calling, and peace in the knowledge that they are not serving alone. May the prayers of His people surround them and sustain them as they shepherd His church.

www.ingramcontent.com/pod-product-compliance
Lightning Source LLC
LaVergne TN
LVHW011052110826
845149LV00015B/3465

9798998834431